SERVICE LEARNING

margit misangyi watts

University of Hawaii at Manoa

Upper Saddle River, New Jersey
Columbus, Ohio

Vice President and Publisher: Jeffery W. Johnston
Executive Editor: Sande Johnson
Editorial Assistant: Lynda Cramer
Production Editor: Alexandrina Benedicto Wolf
Design Coordinator: Diane C. Lorenzo
Cover Designer: Candace Rowley
Cover Photo: Fotosearch
Production Manager: Pamela D. Bennett
Director of Marketing: David Gesell
Marketing Manager: Amy Judd

Copyright © 2007 by Pearson Education, Inc., Upper Saddle River, New Jersey 07458.
Pearson Prentice Hall. All rights reserved. Printed in the United States of America. This publication is protected by Copyright and permission should be obtained from the publisher prior to any prohibited reproduction, storage in a retrieval system, or transmission in any form or by any means, electronic, mechanical, photocopying, recording, or likewise. For information regarding permission(s), write to: Rights and Permissions Department.

Pearson Prentice Hall™ is a trademark of Pearson Education, Inc.
Pearson® is a registered trademark of Pearson plc
Prentice Hall® is a registered trademark of Pearson Education, Inc.

Pearson Education Ltd.
Pearson Education Singapore Pte. Ltd.
Pearson Education Canada, Ltd.
Pearson Education–Japan

Pearson Education Australia Pty. Limited
Pearson Education North Asia Ltd.
Pearson Educación de Mexico, S.A. de C.V.
Pearson Education Malaysia Pte. Ltd.

ISBN 0-13-232201-3

CONTENTS

PREFACE   v

WHAT IS SERVICE LEARNING?   1
    Connecting Theory and Practice, 3

WHY SERVICE LEARNING?   5
    Goals of Service Learning, 6

WHAT'S IN IT FOR ME?   7
    Personal Growth, 8
    Social Development, 8
    Intellectual Development, 9

WHAT'S IN IT FOR THE COMMUNITY?   11

HOW DO I LEARN WHEN I PARTICIPATE?   13
    Academic Learning, 13
    Personal Development, 13
    Program Improvement, 14
    Reflection, 14
    Reflective Questions, 15
    Journals, 16
    Portfolios, 17

WHAT ARE SOME PROJECT IDEAS?   19
    Case Study: Collaboratory, 21
    Case Study: Online Course, 25
    Case Study: Literacy at Lincoln, 28
    Case Study: E-zine, 31
    Case Study: Kid's Kitchen, 34

HOW DO I GET STARTED?	**37**
FORMS	**39**
IDEAS FOR ASSIGNMENTS	**57**
READING POSSIBILITIES	**59**

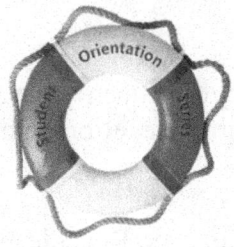 # PREFACE

The need for a booklet on service learning is a testimony to the changes in higher education. More and more faculties across the country are integrating a variety of service-learning projects into their curriculum to actively engage students in their educational endeavors. They are beginning to understand the value of connecting theory to practice. Additionally, student reflections on their service-learning activities document their growth in understanding the diverse communities in which they live. Thus, this booklet provides a starting point for those beginning to integrate service learning. For those already involved, it provides more examples, brings together theoretical information, and offers students a basic guide to the work they are doing.

The pamphlet includes definitions; provides an overview on the impact service learning has on students, faculty, and the community; and discusses the students' personal growth and social and intellectual development. There is a comprehensive list of suggestions for projects within most academic disciplines. The booklet also contains numerous forms—from applications to evaluations—which students and their instructors can use throughout a course.

Hopefully, this booklet provides a blueprint for students as they navigate their way through various service-learning experiences. Though helpful to faculty, it serves primarily as a resource to students involved in service learning.

Acknowledgments

My special thanks to the many students who, over a period of fifteen years, confirmed for me that the value of service learning was worth the effort and commitment of integrating into the curriculum.

Additional thanks to Janette Thomas at Alfred State College, Suzanne Rocheleau at Drexel University, and Jennifer Rosti at Roanoke College for taking the time to enrich this booklet through their contributions and instructive comments.

Finally, much gratitude always goes to my editor, Sande Johnson, and her wonderful team at Prentice-Hall.

margit misangyi watts

SERVICE LEARNING

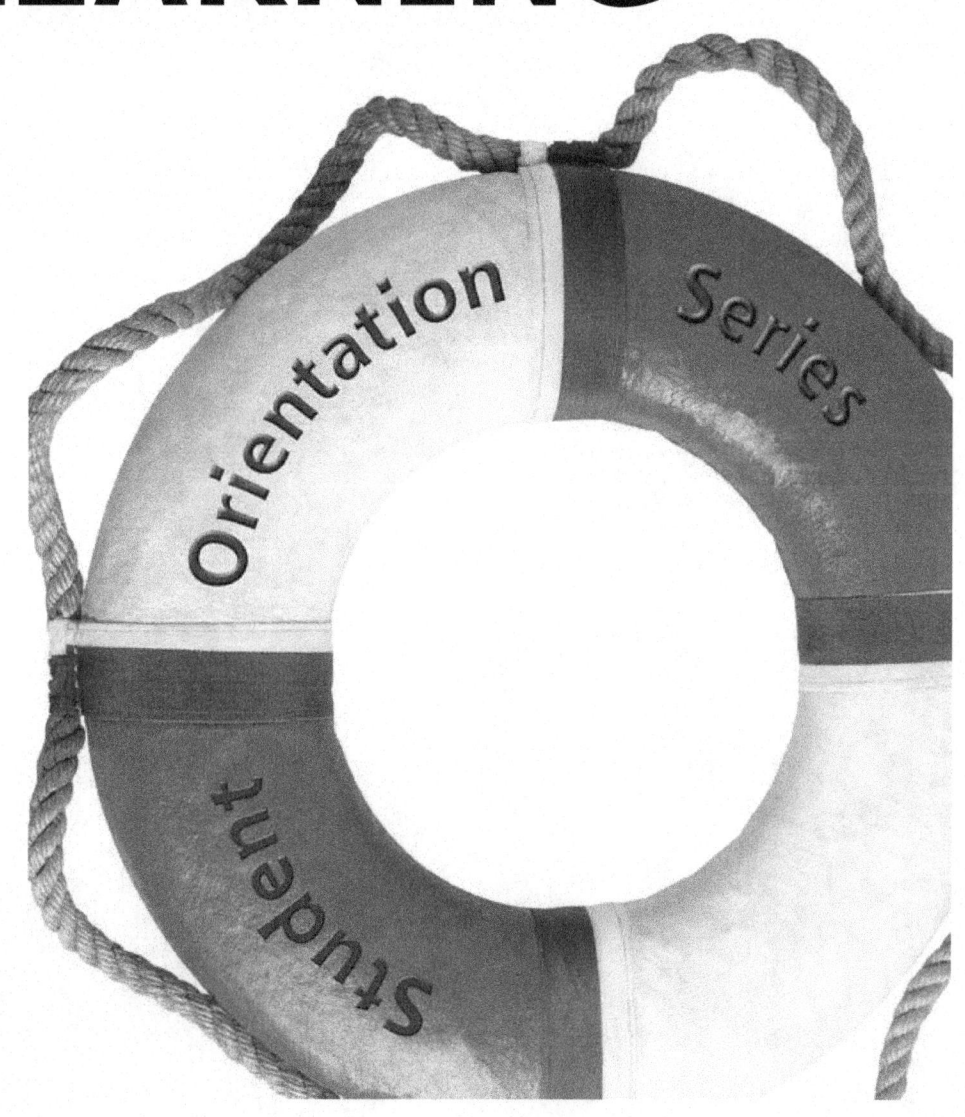

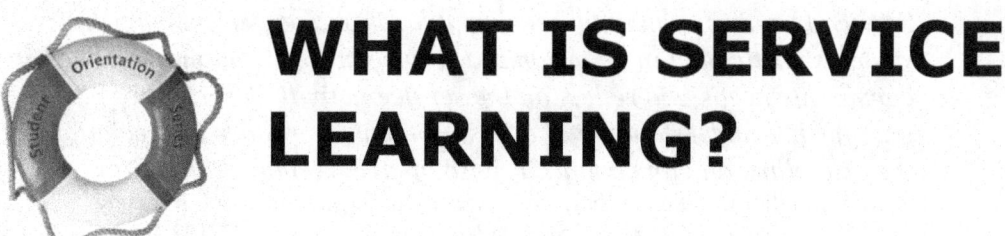

WHAT IS SERVICE LEARNING?

Service, combined with learning, adds value to each and transforms both.

Jane Kendall

Consider the following definitions. You will find similarities among them, even though they have been developed by different organizations.

Service-learning is a method through which citizenship, academic subjects, skills, and values are taught. It involves active learning—drawing lessons from the experience of performing service work.
Developed by the Corporation on National and Community Service as part of their briefing materials for national community service.

Service-learning means a method under which students learn and develop through thoughtfully-organized service that: is conducted in and meets the needs of a community and is coordinated with an institution of higher education, and with the community; helps foster civic responsibility; is integrated into and enhances the academic curriculum of the students enrolled; and includes structured time for students to reflect on the service experience.
American Association for Higher Education (AAHE): Series on Service-Learning to the Disciplines (adapted from the National and Community Service Trust Act of 1993)

Service-learning is a teaching method which combines community service with academic instruction as it focuses on critical, reflective thinking and civic responsibility. Service-learning programs involve students in organized community service that addresses local needs, while developing their academic skills, sense of civic responsibility, and commitment to the community.
Community College National Center for Community Engagement

> *Service-learning is a credit-bearing, educational experience in which students participate in an organized service activity that meets identified community needs and reflect on the service activity in such a way as to gain further understanding of course content, a broader appreciation of the discipline, and an enhanced sense of civic responsibility.*
> Robert Bringle and Julie Hatcher, "A Service Learning Curriculum for Faculty." *The Michigan Journal of Community Service Learning.* Fall 1995: 112-122.

> *Service-learning is the various pedagogies that link community service and academic study so that each strengthens the other. The basic theory of service-learning is Dewey's: the interaction of knowledge and skills with experience is key to learning.*
> Thomas Ehrilich, In Barbara Jacoby and Associates. *Service-Learning in Higher Education: Concepts and Practices.* San Francisco, CA: Jossey-Bass, 1996.

From the various definitions presented, you can see that the key concept is that service learning is an educational model which combines experiential learning and community service. Additionally, guided by faculty and community leaders, students participate in planning and executing service projects, which in turn are tied to their academic curricula.

Quite often, students equate service learning with community service. Many high schools require some form of community service before graduation. Some of these activities include cleaning up beaches and parks, reading to the elderly, and tutoring children in elementary schools. These activities are certainly similar to the kinds of projects that are found in service learning. What makes them different is that they are usually not connected to a particular course or subject area. The community service is viewed as a way to build character, teach ethics, and foster civic responsibility.

The call for service in an educational setting is a call for practical experience to enhance learning and to reinforce moral and civic values inherent in serving others. Additionally, service learning offers students the opportunity to be creative problem solvers, be members of a team, synthesize information, and make educated and informed decisions.

Experiential learning is "learning by doing" or education in action. One form of experiential learning is an internship—the student goes out into the community and works with an agency or company to learn about the various aspects of a particular profession. What differentiates an internship from service learning? Internships are geared toward helping reinforce career choices for students. Service learning entails both service to the community and making connections to the academic courses that support the experience—its purpose is not primarily career-oriented.

In service learning, you gain the educational experience of actively working in an organized service that meets some community need. This work will be integrated into your academic curriculum and enriches your coursework. Finally, the skills you acquire in real-life situations extend your learning from the classroom into your community.

Connecting Theory and Practice

Service learning connects theory and practice. Your experiences will provide the context and framework so you can better understand the more abstract coursework you will encounter. You may wonder how you benefit from the experience. Serving learning:

- **Establishes connections to the community in solving real problems.** When you work with various agencies in the community you participate in developing and/or implementing solutions to problems. The issues you address are not the theoretical ones you read about in your textbooks, but are found in real life and need real-life answers.

- **Helps you see yourself as an integral part of the community.** One of the main goals of education is to help students become productive citizens within their communities. Working in service-learning environments gives you the experience which you can later apply in your own community.

- **Makes you aware of diversity.** When you reach out and spend time in new environments, you can't help but come face-to-face with diverse members of the community.

- **Reinforces democratic values and citizenship.** The whole notion of American democracy is based on a participatory government. Your duty to America as a free citizen is to contribute to the communities in which you live.

- **Helps you learn new skills.** In any new experience you will pick up skills that are new to you; these skills will vary depending on the service-learning site.

- **Allows for non academic strengths to shine.** All students bring a variety of skills, talents, and strengths to any situation. Working in a service-learning environment allows you to share some of your strengths with others—be they organizational, musical, artistic, or other skills.

- **Enhances your academic curriculum.** If you choose carefully, your experiences in service learning will give you insight into the more theoretical work in the classroom.

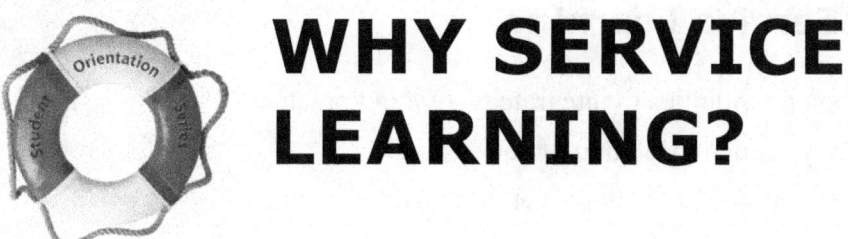

WHY SERVICE LEARNING?

> *I have interacted.*
> *I have maintained a positive attitude.*
> *I have had fun.*
> *I have learned.*
> *I have contributed.*
> *I have helped.*
> *I have fed and nourished children.*
> *I have changed.*
>
> First-year student

Many educational theories have come to the same conclusion: students need to be invested in the process of learning. It has been proven that students learn best when they can either personally relate to what they are learning or can participate in some experiential way. Because of this, many academic institutions across the country are leaning toward requiring service learning. They have discovered that classroom instruction combined with service enhance learning.

Service learning offers you the opportunity to go outside of the classroom; learn about others; find out about their lives, thoughts, and struggles; reflect on what your work means; and finally discover how you fit into your own community.

Goals of Service Learning

- Develop opportunities to integrate theory and practice
- Increase your understanding of social issues
- Teach you to work collaboratively in teams
- Enhance your critical-thinking skills
- Sharpen your problem-solving skills
- Strengthen your sense of social responsibility
- Provide you with a heightened understanding of human differences and commonalities
- Build your self confidence
- Illuminate your personal values and beliefs
- Help you discover a sense of empathy
- Allow you to reflect on what you learned and how it impacts the community

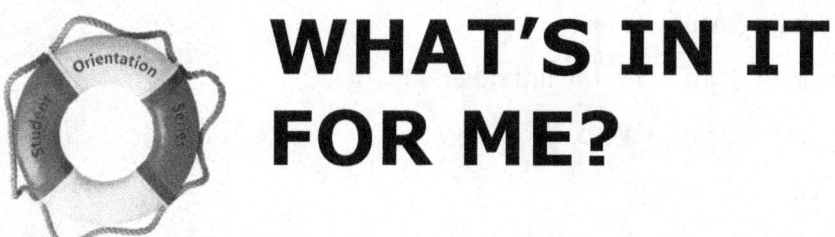

WHAT'S IN IT FOR ME?

> *Experience is not what happens to a man; it is what a man does with what happened to him.*
>
> Aldous Huxley

As a student you are always looking for value due to the time and money spent on your education. So it is appropriate for you to wonder what the benefits—or value added—of your participation in service-learning programs or projects will be.

Here are some outcomes that most educators expect from students who participate in service learning.

- Increased concern for fellow humans
- Ability to problem solve
- Self motivation to learn
- Improved concept of self
- Improved self confidence
- Competence and awareness in new settings
- Responsibility to the community
- Develop a sense of usefulness
- Open to new experiences

- Moral development
- Positive shift in attitudes toward others
- Higher academic achievement
- Tolerance for diversity
- Improved communication with others
- Broader knowledge of career opportunities

As you can see, there are many benefits derived from service learning. Look at the above outcomes and see how they can be divided into a few categories: ***personal growth, social development,*** and ***intellectual development.*** As you work within the community you will also understand the range of jobs available, learn about the skills necessary to do these jobs, develop valuable contacts, and gain experiences that you can include on your résumé.

Personal Growth

Working outside the confines of the classroom challenges you to bring yourself front and center in the community. You need to develop interpersonal communication skills and learn to effectively communicate with a wide range of individuals and groups, both formally and informally. To complete tasks within a community organization, you need to exhibit motivation, personal management skills, interpersonal skills, and resourcefulness.

You will become a better problem solver and, in the process, you increase your self-confidence and can clearly articulate your sense of self (who you are). Service learning also enables you to go outside of the classroom to learn about people whose lives are different from yours; find out about their lives, thoughts, and struggles; reflect on what your presence might mean; and finally, discover who you are. These experiences raise self-esteem, build character, and empower you to see yourself as an integral player in your own community.

Social Development

Another benefit of your participation in service learning is your personal development as a citizen. Social development is crucial to the final product of higher education—an educated citizen. In the process of your work within the community, you learn to accept social responsibility and are providing a service to others. You learn to appreciate, understand, and increase your knowledge of diverse cultures and values.

During the course of your service-learning activities, you learn how to work with others and take responsibility to accomplish tasks as a team. By participating in the community, you begin to see how everyone is interconnected and understand that you are a member of the community with a stake in what happens. Service can even be viewed as a catalyst for social change. For instance, your participation on neighborhood boards may lead to new zoning laws. Finally, you will develop leadership skills, enhancing your ability to work within the community.

Intellectual Development

You will learn to think critically and logically. New educational models suggest that students need to be invested in the learning process: you do your best learning when you can apply knowledge and/or relate it to yourself. Experiences such as service learning can lead to deep and connected learning, and can help students make meaning of their academic learning.

Students will understand how to analyze methods for solving problems. The specific material covered in the course you are taking will be broadened and your understanding of the subject matter will be deepened. Experiences such as service learning increase the complexity of your learning. Most importantly, when you are involved in a service-learning project, you find yourself becoming more interested in the subject matter and more motivated to succeed. You start to clearly understand the importance of your academic work to your life. It is a step toward the educational goal of becoming a lifelong learner.

WHAT'S IN IT FOR THE COMMUNITY?

Everyone can be great, because everyone can serve.

Dr. Martin Luther King, Jr.

Agencies are anxious to draw from the ranks of college students. You are offering them the gift of labor and time to help them achieve their goals.

More importantly, the community invests in the education of its citizens—you. It would like to see its citizens emerge from academia with a sense of social responsibility, an understanding of diverse cultures and value systems, and a commitment to participate in the life of the community they choose to live in after graduation. Additionally, there is the hope that experiential education, such as service learning, helps prepare a well-educated and productive workforce.

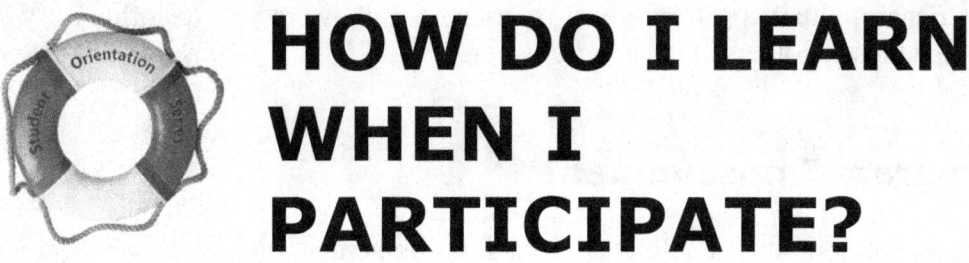

HOW DO I LEARN WHEN I PARTICIPATE?

*I hear and I forget.
I see and I remember.
I do and I understand.*

Chinese Proverb

As you process your daily experiences, you begin to realize your learning potential. Thus, service-learning programs almost always have a major reflective component that is central to the process of learning. Reflection is strongly encouraged because it helps with *academic learning, personal development,* and *program improvement.* Reflection involves observation, asking questions, and making meaning out of your experiences.

Academic Learning

Reflective writing, such as keeping a portfolio or a journal, helps improve your reading and writing skills, helps you understand the course you are taking, and offers you a venue to analyze problems, generate alternatives, and further develop your critical-thinking skills.

Personal Development

Ongoing reflection helps reveal your own personal development—changes in how you perceive the world around you, as well as your own self-image. Articulating these thoughts to yourself and to others helps you take charge of your experiences. Learning from your experiences empowers you to influence your life and those of others in meaningful ways.

Program Improvement

A good reason for including a reflective component in any service-learning program is that it helps improve the program. For example, giving feedback to a program director on the activities you are involved in helps him/her make positive changes in the program. Providing feedback to the community agencies you are working with is an invaluable contribution.

Reflection

Reflection is a process that helps you understand your learning in new ways. It allows you to look back on your experiences and create new knowledge for yourself.

Reflection helps you:

- Think critically about your experiences.
- Link thought to action. Reflection helps you look at your own thinking (metacognition), which helps you decide on future actions.
- Put your experiences into a larger context by thinking about the agency and its place in the community
- Challenge your own attitudes, beliefs, assumptions, privileges, prejudices, and stereotypes.
- Explore policies, laws, trends, and theories.
- Understand your own reactions to your experiences.
- Make sense out of the actions of others. It allows you to look back on what you observed and analyze what happened.
- Improve the quality of your own experience.
- Improve the services of the agency you are working with.

Reflective Questions

Cognitive reflection focuses on the new skills and/or knowledge you have gained from your experiences.

Ask yourself these reflective questions to help you to discover what you've learned.

- Which service learning goals am I accomplishing?
- What challenges am I encountering?
- What new skills am I learning?
- What work am I doing?
- What themes and concepts from my course have become apparent during my work?
- How can I bring my community experience back to the classroom?
- What information do I wish I had?
- How does service learning relate to my course?
- What have I learned this week?
- How can the knowledge I learned in class benefit the community?
- When something occurs at my agency, which concepts from readings or class can help me understand things more clearly?
- How has the community benefited from this activity?

Affective reflection involves learning about your feelings and how your experiences have changed your opinions, perspectives, or attitudes.

Ask yourself these questions to help you explore these issues:

- What did I do today that made me feel I made a difference?
- What in my life has led me to believe a particular thing?
- How do others view me?
- Did I take any risks this week?
- What frustrates or confuses me while I am working in my community?
- Did anything happen that made me feel uncomfortable?

- How do I tell others about my experiences?
- Was I disappointed with my site this week?
- What did someone say that surprised me?
- How have I benefited from my experience this week?

Ask yourself the following questions to help you reflect on the ***process*** of your service-learning experiences and what you have learned from them.

- What is the most difficult part of my work?
- What surprised me about my experience?
- How have my experiences changed my attitude toward communities?
- What did I do, think, hear, feel, and smell on my first day?
- How can I describe my experience? Can I provide as much detail as possible?
- What would I change if I were in charge of the agency?
- How do people at the agency view me?
- What happened at the site while I was there?
- What questions do I have about what they do?
- What insights have I gained into other people's ways of thinking?
- What kind of person is successful at this type of agency?

Journals

There are many ways to optimize your learning. One of the most common methods is keeping a journal. Journals prompt you to keep track of what is happening and your reaction to it, and to think about what it all means. Journal writing captures how you see, experience, understand, react to, and make sense of what you are doing.

Writing down your thoughts helps you:

- Contemplate on the relationship among ideas.
- Consider connections you haven't been aware of before.
- Study the contrasts you experience.

- Understand the implications of what you are doing and seeing.
- See the significance of your service-learning work.
- Make meaning out of the experiences you are having.

Additionally, writing in a journal allows you to:

- Keep an ongoing dialogue with yourself about things that interest you.
- Keep a record of your activities and progress.
- Evaluate your learning and review your reactions.
- Practice personal writing.
- Explore new theories, thoughts, concepts, and ideas.

Your journal will contain snapshots of the sights, smells, concerns, sounds, ideas, doubts, fears, insights, and whatever questions you may have about the people and issues you face in your service-learning experience. It is important to be honest about your thoughts and feelings. A journal is not a log or a time sheet; it is a record of your thoughts, actions, and reactions.

Portfolios

Portfolios are systematic collections of student work that serve as the basis to examine effort, improvement, and processes, as well as illustrate the student's strengths and needs. Most often, portfolios are assessment tools instructors use to monitor the student's ongoing progress. However, portfolios are also useful for the students themselves. They can be vehicles for ongoing self-assessment and reflection wherein students can set goals, see their work take shape over time, and make meaning of their whole work.

What you put into the portfolio is up to you (or your instructor). It can be a compilation of all of your work during a particular semester and for a specific course. Or, it can be a collection of writings, notes, thoughts, and whatever you feel is an accurate illustration of your thoughts and work. Portfolios in their entirety can give you a glimpse into your own learning and the development in your thinking—the skills you acquired during the course of your service-learning experiences and changes in your perceptions, attitudes, and ideas over time.

Keeping a portfolio is easy. You can use a three-ring binder or a special folder set aside for a particular course. You can make copies of electronic journals and emails you sent to your instructor or other students, copies of journals, and copies of assignments and papers written for the course which relate to your service-learning activities.

WHAT ARE SOME PROJECT IDEAS?

> *Never doubt that a small group of thoughtful committed citizens can change the world; indeed, it is the only thing that ever has.*
>
> — Margaret Mead

Over the past twenty years or so, colleges and universities around the country have implemented myriad projects for students in their communities. These varied from helping in a soup kitchen to creating websites for non-profit organizations. In this section you will find many examples and ideas to fit your own needs and match a course you are taking. The examples are divided into general disciplinary categories and miscellaneous categories.

Though many of the project ideas that follow appear to be long-term commitments, it is easy to find projects that are short term or one-time experiences. These projects often address a community need, which could eventually lead to long-term involvement.

Service Learning

Accounting

- Develop an accounting system for a non-profit organization
- Instruct residents of a halfway house or other similar facility in personal finance
- Help obtain financing for a community project
- Work in schools with high school students to prepare them for college financial needs and other life skills for everyday living
- Assist in the staffing of a community cooperative store
- Help indigent and elderly citizens with tax preparation

Agriculture

- Gardening projects for elementary students
- Work with the elderly on growing vegetables and/or the establishing common gardens
- Organize and/or participate in a food program
- Develop educational materials on nutrition
- Assist your local Foodbank or other outreach programs in distributing food

Anthropology

- Work with the elderly to write their histories
- Create traveling programs to share stories, plays, food, and other items for cultural groups
- Prepare displays in schools or public libraries related to community history
- Help senior citizens create their family tree
- Create oral histories by interviewing community leaders who are now retired but have much to share

CASE STUDY

Collaboratory

This was an initiative included as part of a foundation course for a learning community. The project brought together teams of college and K–12 students, museum staff, faculty, and others from around the country to create museum exhibits reflecting research on a theme. This was not a traditional service-learning setting. Service-learning students reached out to K–12 students and helped them participate in a large research project, which was later shown to the public.

> *By doing this project it really brought out part of me that I didn't know was in me.*
>
> First-year student

Students were connected over electronic mail and became members of Walden3, a virtual community that provided a text-based platform for world-building and synchronous communication. It provided an online venue for team members to access each other, as well as museum staff, librarians, and faculty.

One important component of **Collaboratory** was that it encouraged students to recognize learning as an ongoing endeavor; that education is as much a process as a product; and that connecting to the rest of the world broadens perspectives, enhances creativity, and nurtures intellectual inquiry.

> *I have learned so much about myself. I have learned so much about others. I have learned what it means to give. I have learned what it means to help. I have learned the meaning of the phrase, "do something." I have learned what it means to be patient. And I have learned not to take life for granted.*
>
> First-year student

"Celebrations" was the theme for one particular year. The goal was for students to learn a number of research strategies in their foundation course and then collaborate with K–12 students. Students worked in teams and did extensive research on the origins of various celebrations

Service Learning

from around the world. They created "pathfinders"—outlines of research possibilities for each of the celebrations. These pathfinders included research questions; reviews of the literature, methodologies, annotated bibliographies; and intended outcomes for the research. However, rather than complete a traditional research paper, the students worked with their K–12 and college partners to create exhibits. These exhibits were put on display at the natural history museum.

Archeology

- Work with your local museum to catalog artifacts
- Work with a local genealogy society to study cemeteries
- Help local contractors as they excavate possible burial sites

Architecture

- Help the needy with home improvement projects
- Design a corner of a playground or a gathering spot
- Initiate a historic building preservation program
- Design a community center for senior citizens
- Plan the renovation of a community site in need
- Find emergency housing for those in need

Arts

- Work with children in local schools on art projects and teach them new techniques
- Offer music lessons after school
- Partner with your neighborhood museum, shopping malls, and other groups/organizations to have them display the work of local public school students
- Find an open space to create a community mural

- Volunteer at galleries, gallery events, theater and dance projects, and other cultural events
- Develop short theater presentations for local schools
- Help tutor students in any of the arts
- Present free concerts for the elderly and for local public schools
- Design murals to beautify schools and parks

Biology/Botany

- Work with teachers in local public schools to develop school gardens and pocket parks
- Conduct classes in senior centers on the biology of aging
- Organize a group to lobby for better medical attention for low income citizens, the elderly, and other special needs groups
- Assist neighborhoods to safely eradicate pests
- Study nutritional practices in day care centers and then develop educational materials for parents
- Work with the department of education to conduct presentations on the pathology of AIDS, HIV infection, and other sexually-transmitted diseases
- Work as volunteers at nature centers or for ecological and environmental groups in your area

Business

- Organize workshops on how to start a business; provide counseling and individual planning
- Assist non-profit organizations with audits and other financial needs
- Create marketing strategies for community organizations
- Help non-profit organizations develop contracts and other business-related forms
- Create business plans for students
- Develop or participate in a consumer hotline for your community
- Volunteer with a group that provides help in solving consumer problems

Chemistry

- Assist your community in its fight against drug abuse
- Publish information about the hazards of drugs, alcohol, and nicotine
- Work with community agencies to develop nutritional food plans
- Monitor pollutants in your community and then lobby state government to keep the air and water clean
- Support chemical/poison recycling projects
- Participate in residential water testing for homes and wells

Computer Sciences and Technology

- Work with teachers in schools to help students master various computer skills
- Establish a computer rehabilitation/recycling program in your community
- Create public service announcements for TV and radio
- Create a cable television show with students
- Offer to videotape projects and events hosted by community organizations
- Create websites for non-profit organizations
- Provide training opportunities for adults who need computer skills
- Develop computerized learning modules to be used by students
- Offer time in community centers to help train senior citizens
- Design promotional videos for non-profit agencies
- Work with your local library and run mini-computer literacy workshops

CASE STUDY

Online Course

Most faculty and staff at higher-learning institutions grapple with limited time and personnel as they try to develop a new program. Sometimes, the organizational structure itself gets in the way of new ideas and projects. Thus, the concept of an online component and structure for service learning might be a good option.

An e-learning environment makes resources easily accessible to students and helps them explore and develop their information literacy and technological skills. For teachers who don't think they have the time to include service learning, this electronic environment offers choices for integration.

By giving most of the responsibility to the students, and by putting the readings and reflective components of the course online, the projects can be varied and successful.

In one such instance, students were asked to read a number of selections placed on a course website. The students were then responsible for gathering additional information about service learning in general, as well as specific issues relevant to their community agency. The information was then shared on the website. Each week students wrote reflective e-journals to document how they spent their two hours at the agency of their choice.

Thus, rather than conduct a project in which the entire class was involved, the students chose from among over forty community agencies in setting up a working relationship throughout the semester.

The mission of the program to involve students within the community was well-served. Additionally, the students were able to build their research skills by searching for relevant articles and materials to be shared with the class.

As a final project, each student conducted research for their particular agency, and then did a poster presentation of their results and conclusions.

Economics

- Produce materials for low-income families to help with their finances
- Help plan a fundraising dinner for a non-profit agency or youth group
- Do a comparative survey of food prices at local stores and publish a pamphlet advising community members of the best prices
- Help low-income families determine a workable budget
- Set up a work referral project to help teens find jobs
- Organize community business to come together and brainstorm on how to better employ members within the community
- Arrange training for the unemployed members of your community to help them attain employable skills

Education

- Bring senior citizens and elementary school children together to share their stories; help develop a grandparent program for schools or pre-schools
- Work with teachers to develop lesson plans
- Implement after-school activities
- Plan and organize a Teacher Appreciation Day
- Provide child care or elder care for people who are looking for work or attending school
- Develop literacy programs and adult-education programs in community centers
- Organize educational programs for inmates
- Participate in language-acquisition programs for immigrants
- Tutor children at all levels
- Organize a book drive and then create a community-based library
- Tutor recent immigrants and help them with basic tasks
- Organize and/or create a tutoring center at a particular school
- Work with the local school board to find out community needs
- Publish pamphlets and other materials for high school students to help them prepare for their first year in college

Engineering

- Create playground equipment for children with disabilities
- Create walkers for the elderly
- Design better shower assistance for home-care facilities
- Work with environmental agencies to design efficient waste disposal, compost makers, solar energy panels, and the like
- Work with local architects to help design community gathering spaces
- Assist with middle- and high-school robotics programs

English/Journalism

- Help non-profit organizations develop, publish, and sustain newsletters for their members
- Work with senior citizens to document their stories; donate these stories to the local library
- Volunteer to help judge school essay contests, history day activities, or science fair events
- Read to children in schools and in after-school programs
- Study current issues and write/publish stories to bring that information to others
- Write articles for community and school publications
- Help people with disabilities write letters
- Assist elementary school children in their writing by helping them create their own books; donate these books to a local children's hospital
- Write letters to the editor in support of a particular cause
- Establish a magazine in support of a community endeavor
- Organize letter writing campaigns
- Create an adult-literacy project or volunteer in ongoing programs
- Create brochures and fund-raising proposals for non-profit organizations

CASE STUDY

Literacy at Lincoln

This project allowed service learning students to work with children and conduct research by mentoring at an elementary school. The focus was on helping improve reading skills. College students went to Lincoln Elementary School each week to read with and to the students. In their college course they researched the concept of literacy and the multiple programs that have been developed over the years. Doing this research helped them design the methods they would use with the elementary students.

In addition, volunteers worked with the food bank to assemble food boxes monthly. These were distributed to the families in the Lincoln Elementary neighborhood. This work helped connect the college students with both the children and their families, giving them insight into the socio-economic status of these children.

The ability to reach out into the community exemplified the prevailing pedagogy of the program, which was to link the research skills they were learning to some aspect of the community they lived in. Students needed to reflect on their own values, investigate differing viewpoints encountered in the literature, and maintain a journal or log of activities.

Environmental Studies

- Conduct surveys of air quality in care homes, public spaces, and work spaces
- Experiment with water samples from your local lake or river to study possible pollutants
- Clean up a stream bed, marshlands, neighborhood blight areas, or roadsides
- Beautify a park or create a small park
- Work with your state or city park office and help restore nature trails, rebuild bridges, or remove non-indigenous plants

- Develop bike lanes and walking trails
- Develop a brochure on low impact hiking and camping
- Work with local nurseries to plan a "Plant a Tree Day"
- Organize a neighborhood clean-up day(s), campus clean-ups, or beautification programs for local schools
- Develop a kiosk for nature trails in your community
- Work with the community on erosion control and habitat management
- Compile lists of flora and fauna in your area
- Participate in campaigns for better crosswalks, bike lanes, and so forth
- Do a study of your community traffic patterns
- Document incidents of lead poisoning or other hazardous materials found in public areas
- Develop brochures for parents and residents in neighborhoods that deal with the potential of lead poisoning

Ethnic Studies

- Organize ethnic awareness days
- Tutor people whose second language is English
- Study the different needs of the diverse cultures in your community
- Organize a festival honoring the cultural diversity in your community
- Volunteer in existing programs related to homelessness, hunger, etc. in specific communities where you have language/communication skills

Geography/Cultural Geography

- Create neighborhood maps
- Work with children in schools to help them understand their geographical location
- Tutor students in school
- Develop after-school projects which focus on the geography of your community
- Create a website detailing the various geographical locations of specific stores, agencies, parks, and other public places

Health and Recreation

- Organize a community health fair
- Work with schools on documenting dental, vision, and auditory needs of students
- Plan health and nutrition activities for after-school programs
- Create and/or volunteer in a fitness program for adults with disabilities
- Gather medical data regarding vaccinations, etc.
- Organize activities to raise funds for community parks and recreational events
- Set up a buddy program with local schools to collect and provide food (snack items) on weekends for needy students

History

- Document the history of your town
- Plan a community parade or a tour of historic buildings
- Do a survey of historical sites in your town and publish your findings
- Have students "adopt a grandparent" and learn their history
- Create a celebration for your town or neighborhood school
- Research ethnographic topics and make your results available to appropriate agencies
- Work with an agency to help them write their own history
- Publish a journal, or create a website, that highlights the uniqueness of your community
- Set up events and workshops to teach the community about its history
- Work with schoolchildren to help them discover the history of their own families

CASE STUDY

E-zine

If it is not possible for students go out into the community for their service learning, creating an E-zine may fit the bill. In one learning community, students were urged to research the first-year experience—everything from living in dorms to getting lost on the first day of class. They brought this material back to class, shared it with their classmates, and then developed a plan to create E-zine, an online magazine.

E-zine included articles on the first-year experience, tips for getting ready to come to college, suggestions for study aids and groups, lists of places to eat and gather, and other relevant topics. This online magazine was then shared with all of the local high schools. Juniors and seniors were given some firsthand insight into what they are to expect in their near future.

Languages

- Work with immigrants to teach them the English language
- Volunteer as a translator in schools, hospitals, or community centers
- Work as a bilingual aide in public schools
- Volunteer to help non-profit organizations translate their material into several languages appropriate for your particular community

Law

- Develop community workshops on legal rights
- Operate a legal assistance program
- Develop student courts in the schools
- Assist victims of crime, abused women and children, and the homeless
- Create crime-prevention brochures

- Develop a conflict-management program within the community
- Advise community organizations on matters of liability
- Provide paralegal assistance to minors, minorities, and immigrants
- Assist grassroots groups
- Study laws and regulations regarding nursing homes and then help them with compliance
- Volunteer in your community ombudsman program

Mathematics

- Tutor students in schools and provide extended college preparation support
- Provide tax preparation assistance/support for those in need

Music

- Document the indigenous music of your community
- Organize a concert performed by children or for children
- Develop music therapy programs for children and senior citizens
- Stage musical performances at community centers
- Provide recitals and events at adult daycare facilities, convalescent facilities, and retirement communities
- Raise funds to purchase instruments for children from low-income families

Philosophy

- Take the basic questions of philosophy into elementary and high schools
- Work with the elderly on ethical and moral considerations
- Help at-risk students think about social reform and cultural diversity
- Connect theoretical course readings with time spent working within the community

Physics

- Develop devices that help the elderly with day-to-day activities
- Create solar heating systems for non profit organizations
- Tutor K–12 students

Political Science

- Organize a voter registration drive
- Work with local politicians on various issues
- Work with groups to lobby for particular legislation that affects senior citizens, immigrants, abused women, and at-risk youth
- Serve on a neighborhood board
- Support candidates who take a stand on human rights issues
- Organize a fair to help people better understand the politics of their particular community
- Educate children about democracy and the gift of voting
- Assist action groups

Psychology

- Assist the mental health organizations in your community
- Establish and/or create a crisis hotline
- Work with the Ronald McDonald House to support families of children in crisis or in the hospital
- Work with at-risk children in the school system
- Assist with counseling programs for families
- Help out in your local mental care facilities
- Offer assistance in spousal abuse centers
- Participate in after-school programs for young adolescents
- Work with special-needs agencies in your community
- Assist with counseling alcoholics
- Help publish materials for agencies that deal with drugs and alcohol abuse
- Work in drug abuse clinics

CASE STUDY

Kid's Kitchen

Kids' Kitchen, a community service project, was a partnership between the local Rotary Club, the local Foodbank, and college students. The Rotarians donated monies to pay for a site coordinator and helped the site with painting, building, and other activities as needed.

> *I have interacted. I have maintained a positive attitude. I have had fun. I have learned. I have contributed. I have helped. I have fed and nourished the minds and stomachs of some children. I have changed.*
> — First-year student

Kids' Kitchen provided meals for young children who were alone after school. Up to 35 children, ages 5 to 12, were offered meals each day. The school principal worked closely with the coordinator of the program to facilitate communication with the families. In the late afternoon every Monday through Friday, meals were prepared and served to the children. Additionally, the first-year students became role models for these children. They encouraged youngsters to participate in various tabletop and recreational activities. The school children were also given opportunities to sit and "talk story," got help with their homework, and participated in lively discussions. Thus, volunteers not only supervised the children during their meals, but also nourished the youngsters' minds. Students who participated in Kids' Kitchen had life changing experiences.

> *If I can change one kid's life, I can change the future.*
> — First-year student

This project was a more traditional service-learning project in that students actually went to the site, served food, and mentored young children. The articulation with the curriculum was through the research course. Students were conducting research on topics related to their work at Kid's Kitchen. They became aware of the economic, legal, and social issues that arise when working with a community, especially children from low-income families. Much of their learning came from the reflective journals they kept throughout the semester. They were able to make connections with what they were doing at the site and the reading they were doing in many of their general education classes (sociology, political science, and psychology).

Religion

- Organize informational programs for PTA's and other organizations to help raise awareness of positive inter-denominational activities
- Help organize interfaith activities for the youth
- Volunteer at a church of your choice with any of their activities

Social Work

- Volunteer with a family violence support group
- Volunteer in foster care programs in your community
- Help create awareness of child neglect issues
- Research the status of welfare recipients in your neighborhoods

Sociology

- Develop awareness within your community on the need for halfway houses
- Conduct a clothing drive for community members in need
- Study the density of your community and the problems arising from this
- Establish a network of volunteer services for your community
- Assess community needs and then join the appropriate agency to address those needs
- Work with a parent group on a school or park improvement project
- Research community needs and publish your reports
- Study the homeless in your community and create programs to help them

Speech

- Volunteer to help students prepare for high school speech contests
- Offer to judge debates and speeches at schools
- Participate in school theater rehearsals
- Meet with special interest groups and help them develop skills to publicize their projects and gather public support

Women's Studies

- Volunteer to support a spouse abuse center or create support projects, such as gathering clothes or toiletry items for women
- Help develop or support a crisis hotline for women
- Research employment opportunities for women
- Help young women in areas of math and science
- Help organize a back-to-work program for single mothers
- Set up a daycare center to support women looking for work

Zoology

- Volunteer at your local animal shelter
- Volunteer to work with zoologists at your local zoo
- Develop programs in schools to teach children about animals
- Put together a daycare center for pets
- Volunteer at animal rescue projects
- Create awareness and collect funds for specific groups
- Foster animals from your local SPCA animal shelter

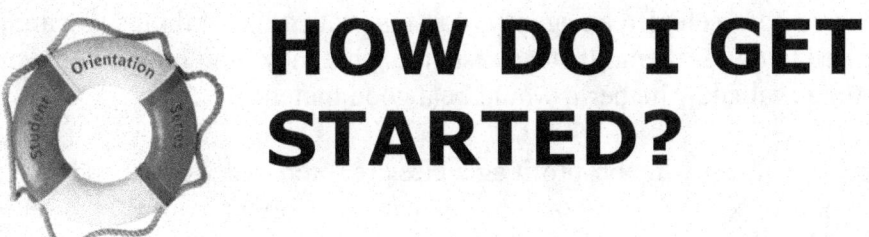

HOW DO I GET STARTED?

---

*We are what we repeatedly do.
Excellence, then, is not an act,
but a habit.*

Aristotle

Most often your instructor will either suggest potential service-learning activities or organize a service-learning project for your class. However, there are times when an instructor includes service learning into a course and expects students to find appropriate activities. The list presented in the preceding section will help you find an activity that you can adapt to your community and to the needs of your particular class.

If you are on your own for a good part of the service-learning project, you will benefit from the following guidelines:

♦ Before you contact an agency, do some research: Are they a registered non-profit organization? Does a church or an umbrella organization, such as United Way, sponsor them?

♦ Determine your college's or university's policies on doing service-learning activities.

♦ Before you contact an agency, write down your objectives. Be able to articulate what you want to learn.

♦ Find out what the agency's goals are, what they actually do in their day-to-day work, and whether they are looking for volunteers.

- Once you have selected an agency, don't go with a list of things you are prepared to do for them. Instead, listen to what they might need from you and then evaluate whether it would be a good match.

- Be patient. People in non-profit agencies are often overworked and busy. It might take several forms of communication before you are able to set up an appointment and actually begin your talks.

- Be sure to take notes when you finally get a chance to meet with someone. You don't want to walk away with any misunderstandings regarding their goals and expectations.

- Be clear about your own expectations and goals so that you can effectively work with your chosen agency and mutually benefit from the experience.

- Most often, agencies will ask you to participate in an orientation program/meeting so you are familiar with their projects and personnel. Be sure to show up for this meeting; it is an essential component of a good partnership.

- Honestly tell them how much time you are able to invest with the program. Once you both agree on your work hours, always be prompt. If you cannot make it, call in advance. These community agencies are counting on your work.

- Develop a service-learning agreement that you, your instructor, and an agency representative will sign. This makes the expectations official and gives everyone a role to play in the partnership that is being created. (An example of such an agreement is available in the **Forms** section.)

- Check on the legal liabilities that might be a part of your work at the agency. You might want to fill out a Risk, Release and Waiver Form that is specific to your college or university. (Sample in **Forms** section)

FORMS

There are many ways to set up a service-learning project with a community agency. This section provides forms that you can use in your service-learning experiences. You can change or modify these forms to meet the needs of your particular course or agency.

- Service Learning: Preparation

- Service Learning: Reflection

- Contact Information

- Service Learning Contracts

- Student Volunteer Application

- Community Interest Survey

- Service Learning Timesheet

- Assumption of Risk, Release and Waiver Form: Sample (Your college or university should have their own official form for your use.)

- Site Coordinator Evaluation of Student Volunteer

- Volunteer Evaluation Form

- Self-Evaluation Forms

Service Learning: Preparation

Name _____

Agency _____

Date _____

Awareness of the purpose of the service
- Who will this project help?

Application to your education
- Will this project help you understand things in your schoolwork?

- Will the things you learn in school help you do this project? How?

Responsibility to the community
- What would you like to do to help the organization?

Impact on your life
- Do you feel good about partnering with this agency? Why?

- Do you think you will do anything differently after you do this project? If yes, what?

Critical Thinking
- Will this project give you any ideas about how to help other organizations? What?

- Do other people have different perspectives on the agency you have chosen?

- How can you tell whose ideas are best?

Definitions
- Service learning means _____

- Your organization is _____

Service Learning: Reflection

Name _____

Agency _____

Date _____

What?

- What did you do for your project?
- What new areas of your community did you explore?
- Whom did you talk with, help, or work for?
- Did you like the people who worked with you on the project? Why?
- Did you do anything that you have never done before? Describe?

So What?

- How did you feel about doing the project?
- Were there things about the project that you did not like? Describe?
- Did this project actually help anyone? Who?
- Do you think that anyone cared that you worked on this project?
- Did this project help you understand things in your courses? What?
- Did the things you learned in your classes help you in the project? How?

Now What?

- Now that you have done the project, can you see yourself doing it again?
- Will this experience help you in some way?
- In response to your work on this project, do you think you will do anything differently in your life?
- Is there anything you would like to do to help your agency?
- Do you want to keep working on these kinds of community projects?
- Could you now teach others about service learning?

Definitions

- Service learning means _____
- Your organization is _____

Contact Information

PERSONAL INFORMATION

Name _____

Social Security Number or Student ID Number _____

Date of Birth _____

Home and/or Permanent Address _____

_____

Telephone _____ Cell _____ Email _____

The best time to call is: _____

List any previous volunteer experience

_____

_____

_____

EMERGENCY CONTACT INFORMATION

Name _____ Relationship _____

Day Phone _____ Evening Phone _____

_____   _____
              Signature   Date

Service Learning Contract

PERSONAL INFORMATION

Student's Name _____

Address _____

_____

Phone _____ Cell _____

Email _____

Hours/days student is available to work _____

....

SERVICE LEARNING PROGRAM INFORMATION

_____
Name of Service Learning Program/Agency

Address _____

_____

_____   _____
Name of Program/Volunteer Coordinator   Telephone

Hours/days needed by agency _____

_____   _____
Student's Signature   Agency's Signature

Service Learning Contract

This service-learning contract is designed to:

- Help you understand the learning objectives for the course.
- Clarify the activities in which you will be involved and how they relate to the course objectives.
- Ensure that you are aware of your responsibilities for this project.

Student's Name _____

SS# or Student ID _____

Address _____

_____

Phone _____ Cell _____ Email _____

....

PART I SERVICE LEARNING PLAN

Days and times you will work for the agency _____

_____

Proposed Start Date _____ Proposed Completion Date _____

....

PART II LEARNING OBJECTIVES

_____   _____

_____   _____

_____   _____

PART III FINAL AGREEMENT

Student:

I, _____, agree to honor and dependably fulfill the time commitment required for the program I have chosen for my service-learning project. I will participate and successfully complete whatever tasks are necessary to meet my learning goals. I also agree to contact my instructor should I have any concerns or questions about my service-learning experience.

_____   _____
Student's Signature   Date

Program Representative

I, _____, agree to provide adequate training and supervision for the service-learning student, to plan activities for the student within the program which meet the stated learning objectives for the student's course, and to complete necessary service learning forms by due dates. Should there be any concerns about the student(s) working in this agency, I will contact the appropriate instructor.

_____   _____
Representative's Signature   Date

Student Volunteer Application

Student Name _____

Address _____

_____

Telephone _____ Cell _____

Email _____

The best time to call me is: _____

List any previous volunteer experience(s):

_____

_____

_____

....

I am available:

Sunday _____ Thursday _____

Monday _____ Friday _____

Tuesday _____ Saturday _____

Wednesday _____

Community Interest Survey

CHECK THE APPROPRIATE BOX

[ ]   I do see a need for service learners to help in our agency.

[ ]   I do not see a need for student volunteers to help in our program.

If you think that your program would benefit from having students work with you, what are the three areas in which these students could be of most help?

1. _____

2. _____

3. _____

What are the times and days you need help? Also note minimum and maximum hours per week.

MON _____   FRI _____

TUES _____   SAT _____

WED _____   SUN _____

THURS _____

I would like to explore the possibility of using students in our agency. Please call me at _____ between the hours of _____.

_____   _____
Print Name   Date

_____   _____
Signature of Agency Representative   Agency

Service Learning

Service Learning Timesheet

Student Name _____   Course _____

This form serves as your timesheet. Please be sure to get it signed each time you do a service-learning project or spend time at your agency.

DATE	TIME IN	TIME OUT	TOTAL TIME	APPROVAL SIGNATURE

TOTAL HOURS LOGGED _____

Assumption of Risk, Release and Waiver Form

I, _____, understand that there are risks in my participation in *(course name)*, including the risk of PROPERTY DAMAGE, PERSONAL INJURY, OR DEATH. I understand that the state of *(name of your state)*, the *(name of your college or university)*, and their officers, agents, employees, or representatives do not provide liability insurance, or otherwise indemnify me or anyone else who may participate in this project, for any injuries or any other liabilities arising from my service-learning experiences.

Therefore, in consideration of my participation, I assume all risks and responsibilities surrounding the project. I release, agree to defend, hold harmless, and indemnify the *(name of your state)*, the *(name of your college or university)*, and their officers, agents, employees, or representatives from and against all liabilities, claims, demands, or causes of actions, including claims for property damage, personal injury, or death CAUSED BY THE PASSIVE OR ACTIVE NEGLIGENCE OF MYSELF AND/OR THE STATE OF _____, THE (*NAME OF YOUR COLLEGE OR UNIVERSITY*), OR ITS OFFICERS, AGENTS, EMPLOYEES, OR REPRESENTATIVES, for any hidden, latent, or obvious defects in equipment, or cause by any other activities of mine, or anyone else who may be a service learner, volunteer, or participant during this service-learning project.

_____   _____
Signature   Date

_____   _____
Parent or Guardian's Signature   Date
(If participant is under 18 years of age)

Service Learning

Site Coordinator Evaluation of Student Volunteer

Name of Student _____ Date _____

Name of Supervisor _____ Phone _____

Number of Hours Evaluated _____ Number of Days Absent _____

Rating System: 1 = Does not Apply   4 = Average
                 2 = Failing   5 = Above Average
                 3 = Below Average   6 = Excellent

1. **Student reports regularly and punctually.**   1 2 3 4 5 6

2. **Student attends to tasks assigned to him/her.**   1 2 3 4 5 6

3. **Student's clothing and language are appropriate.**   1 2 3 4 5 6

4. **Student works with a positive and willing attitude.**   1 2 3 4 5 6

5. **Student functions alone and does not need to be told what to do.**   1 2 3 4 5 6

6. **Student responds creatively to constructive criticism.**   1 2 3 4 5 6

7. **Student has an accurate sense of his/her own abilities.**   1 2 3 4 5 6

8. **Student solves problems well.**   1 2 3 4 5 6

9. **Student makes an effort to be informed about the agency.**   1 2 3 4 5 6

10. **Student establishes good rapport with agency staff.**   1 2 3 4 5 6

11. **Overall service learning effort of student.**   1 2 3 4 5 6

12. **Additional comments**

_____

_____

I have discussed this evaluation with the student.

_____   _____
Site Coordinator's Signature   Student's Signature

Volunteer Evaluation Form

Date _____

Please rate _____ on each of the characteristics listed by circling the appropriate number. Under Comments, list any of the student's strengths or weaknesses that you feel are important.

1. **Desire and willingness to take on new assignments**
   Fail   1   2   3   4   5   6   7   8   9   10   Excellent

2. **Potential for further development**
   Fail   1   2   3   4   5   6   7   8   9   10   Excellent

3. **Concern for needs of community**
   Fail   1   2   3   4   5   6   7   8   9   10   Excellent

4. **Willingness to work and complete an assignment**
   Fail   1   2   3   4   5   6   7   8   9   10   Excellent

5. **Ability to communicate with teammates**
   Fail   1   2   3   4   5   6   7   8   9   10   Excellent

6. **Creativity and resourcefulness**
   Fail   1   2   3   4   5   6   7   8   9   10   Excellent

7. **Cooperation and willingness to get along with others**
   Fail   1   2   3   4   5   6   7   8   9   10   Excellent

8. **Overall performance**
   Fail   1   2   3   4   5   6   7   8   9   10   Excellent

This volunteer   fails / meets / exceeds   my expectations

COMMENTS

_____

_____

_____
Site Supervisor's Signature

Self-Evaluation Form

Student Name _____

Please take some time to read and reflect on the following questions before completing this Self-Evaluation Form. Remember to answer all questions completely and thoughtfully. Please revise and proofread your evaluation carefully for writing proficiency. Keep a copy for your own records.

1. How did your service-learning experience relate to the class readings, discussions, or activities?

2. How did it make you feel to give your time and energy to others?

3. How did your service-learning work help the community?

4. How has your service-learning experience changed your thinking, attitudes, and actions towards others, yourself, and the community?

5. Do you see yourself staying involved in the community during your college and adult years? Why or why not?

6. What stands out as the best or worst thing that happened to you this semester in your service-learning experience? What did you learn from these experiences?

7. What did you learn about yourself, the people around you, the service site, and/or how your experience relates to your education and the larger issues in society?

8. List any new insights about the service-learning project and/or how it has impacted you personally, academically, or career-wise.

9. Were you satisfied with your experience? Why or why not?

10. What is the most important thing you learned about yourself? About the community? About your course?

11. Have your perceptions of the service-learning experience changed? How?

12. Sum up your service-learning experience in a one- or two-sentence headline.

Self-Evaluation Form

Name _____   Date _____

Please complete this form as honestly as possible. Circle a number on the scale to indicate your answer.

1. **I was able to encourage good rapport in group situations.**

   Very Poor   1   2   3   4   5   Very Good

2. **I was able to encourage good rapport in individual situations.**

   Very Poor   1   2   3   4   5   Very Good

3. **I was able to encourage and participate actively in group activities.**

   Very Poor   1   2   3   4   5   Very Good

4. **I was able to encourage and participate actively with specific individuals.**

   Very Poor   1   2   3   4   5   Very Good

5. **I was able to get involved in activities with little or no prompting.**

   Very Poor   1   2   3   4   5   Very Good

COMMENTS:

_____

_____

_____

IDEAS FOR ASSIGNMENTS

Your instructor has many ideas on how you can make meaning out of your service-learning experiences. However, if you are ever in need of some creative ideas to help you establish the connection between your coursework and the work you are doing within the community, you will find the following assignments helpful and exciting.

Proclamation for a State of Literacy

Write a proclamation (speech) as if you were the king or queen of a country. Address the issue of how you would improve the state of literacy in your kingdom. You should include facts about literacy that have local and/or national impact. These will help highlight the urgency of your message. Be very clear about what you want your people to do about the literacy problem. Make decrees that support your goal of having everyone in the kingdom be able to read.

Be creative. Be a literacy advocate.

This project can be altered to address any topic you are wrestling with in your service project. You could write a proclamation about gay rights, lack of care homes for the elderly, zoning issues in neighborhoods, or any other issue of interest and significance to your work. You might even consider sending an edited version of your proclamation to the editorial page of your local newspaper.

Reflective Self-Assessment Paper

Achievement: Describe any development for which you feel responsible in your agency. Give specific examples of how you know progress was made.

Problematic Events: Describe two problematic events that you experienced during your service-learning activities. State what you would do differently next time.

Career Exploration: Describe what you learned from this project that might affect your professional development and the personal decisions you will make in life.

Purposeful Observation

Several times during the semester you should take the time to be observant and jot down a few pages in your journal.

Make an effort to notice something different each time you are present at your community agency. Listen to those you work with and ask yourself the following questions:

- Why is there a need of my services?

- What is the underlying problem that the agency is addressing? Why does it exist?

- What social, economic, political, and educational systems are maintaining and perpetuating the problem?

- What can I do to work for change?

- How are my courses preparing me to address this or any other problem?

Group Project

Divide the class into groups of five. If possible, divide the students into groups with similar career goals. Each group should select a topic of interest. Students then describe how they would go about arranging for service-learning project that is relevant to their chosen topic.

Details must include how to contact the agency and how to determine agency need, amount of time required for the project, and resources needed, among others. When finished, each group presents to the class what they have developed.

This is a nice way to start thinking about the possibilities for service learning.

READING POSSIBILITIES

Bellah, Robert N. 1995. *Habits of the Heart*. New York: Harper & Row, Publishers.

Coles, Robert. 1993. *The Call of Service*. New York: Houghton Mifflin Company.

Fulwiler, Toby. 1987. *The Journal Book*. Portsmouth: Boynton/Cook Publsihers.

Galura, Joseph A., Pasque, Penny A., Shoem, David, and Howard, Jeffrey (eds.). 2004. *Engaging the Whole of Service-Learning, Diversity, and Learning Communities*. Ann Arbor: OCSL Press at University of Michigan.

Jacoby, Barbara & Associates. 1996. *Service-Learning in Higher Education*. San Francisco: Jossey-Bass Publishers.

Kendall, Jane C. & Associates. 1990. *Combining Service Learning: A Resource Book for Community and Public Service*. North Carolina: National Society for Internships and Experiential Education.

Radest, Howard B. 1993. *Community Service: Encounter with Strangers*. Connecticut: Praeger.

Waterman, Alan S. 1997. *Service-Learning: Applications from the Research*. New Jersey: Lawrence Erlbaum Associates.

Zlotkowski, Edward. 2002. *Service-Learning and the First Year Experience: Preparing Students for Personal Success and Civic Responsibility*. South Carolina: National Resource Center for the First Year Experience & Students in Transition.